Dedication

Coloring book is for coloring artists, who's desire is to make the world more colorful and writers who when they are done coloring the page to write about the content that they have chosen. In dedication, this is for all the blessed families, especially our youth and young at heart as well.

To order additional copies of this book, contact:
Xlibris
1-888-795-4274
www.Xlibris.com
Orders@Xlibris.com

ISBN: 978-1-9845-8194-5 (sc)
ISBN: 978-1-9845-8193-8 (e)

Print information available on the last page

Rev. date: 06/02/2020

So You Think You Can Color?

ILLUSTRATION FOR THOSE WHO COLOR

By

JULIAN VAN DYKE

Writing About What I Colored...

Writing About What I Colored...

Writing About What I Colored...

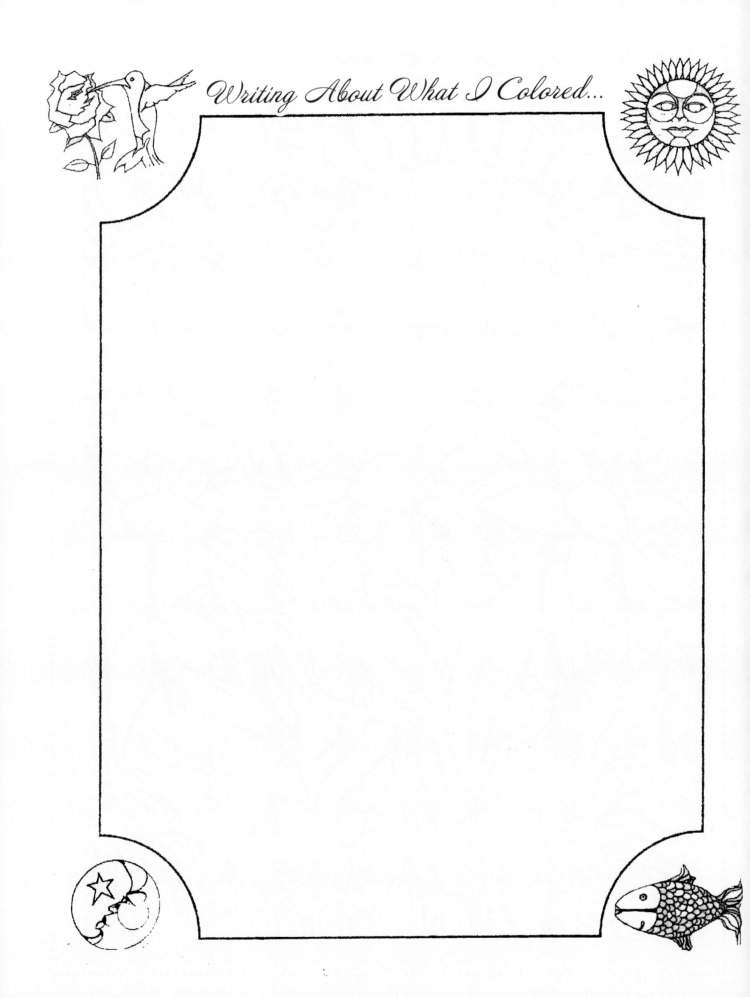

Writing About What I Colored...

Writing About What I Colored...

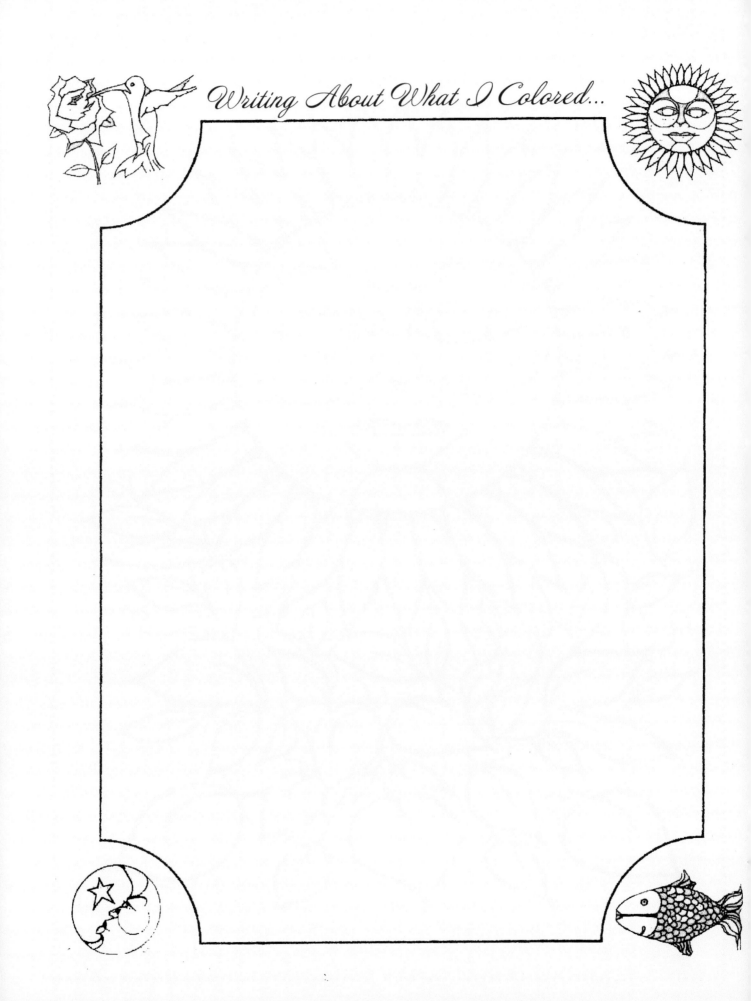

Writing About What I Colored...

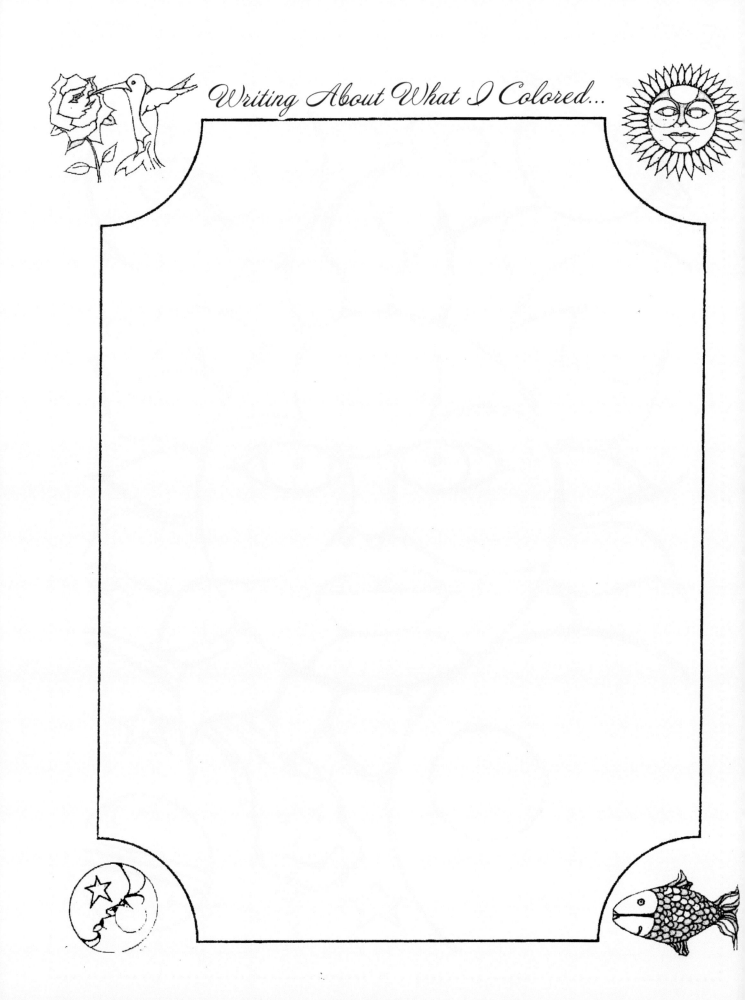

Writing About What I Colored...

Writing About What I Colored...

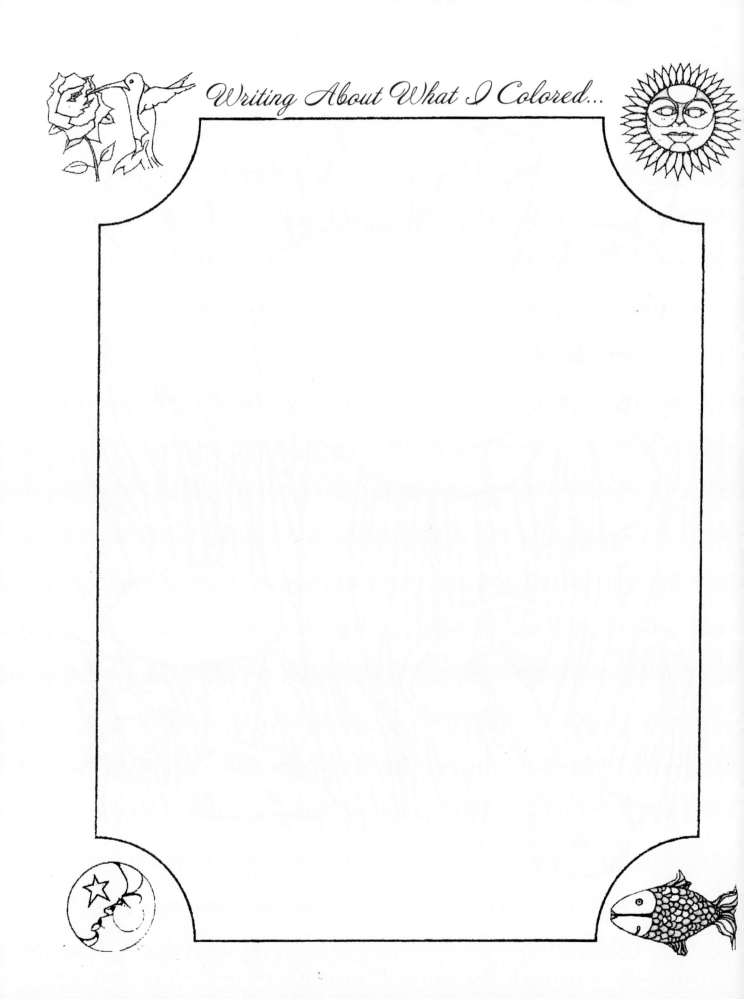

Writing About What I Colored...

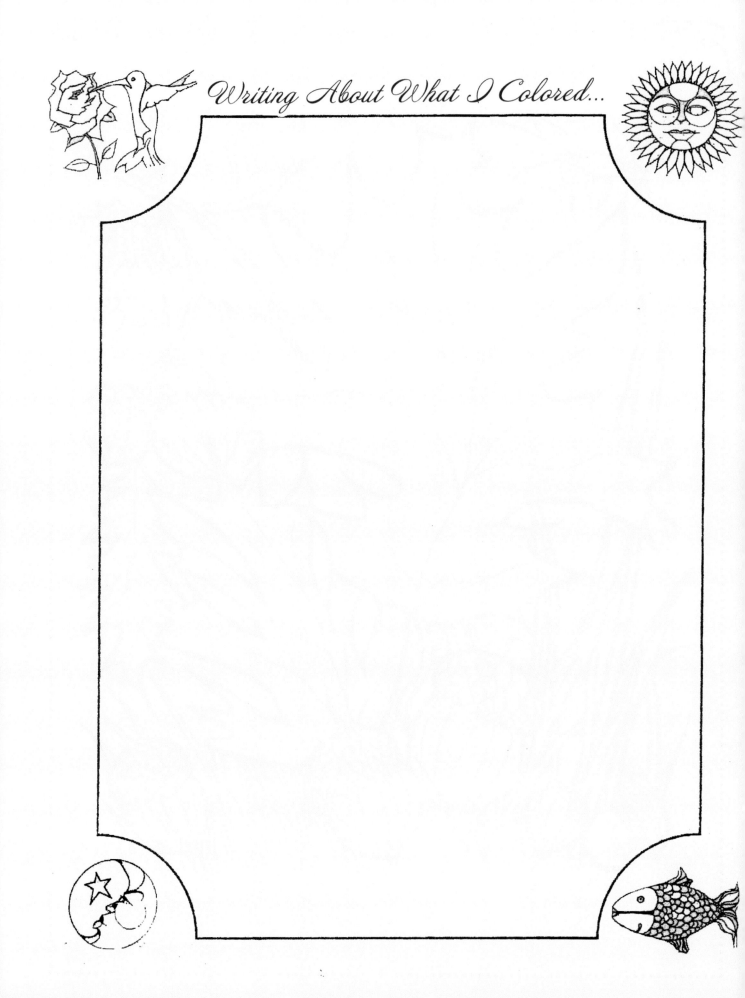

Writing About What I Colored...

Writing About What I Colored...

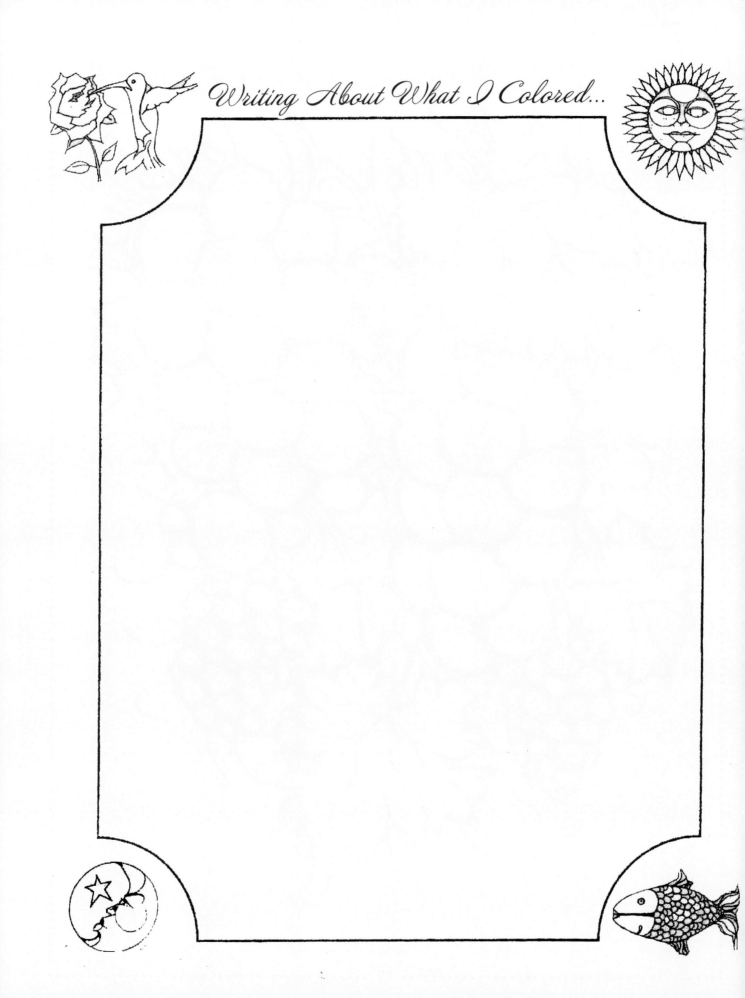

Writing About What I Colored...

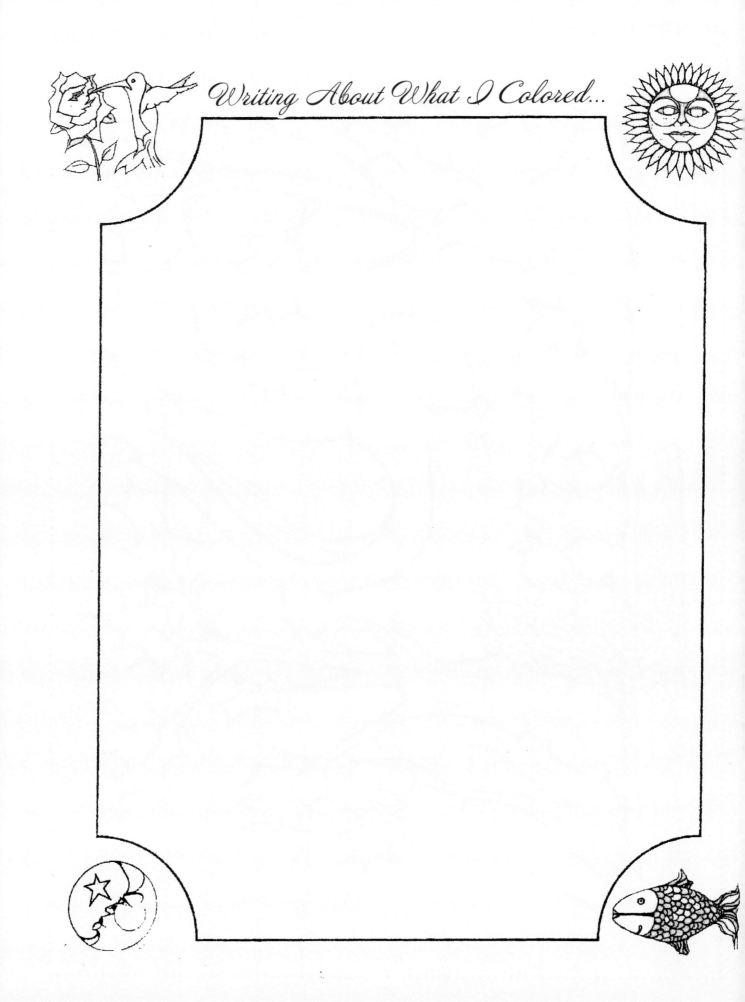

Writing About What I Colored...

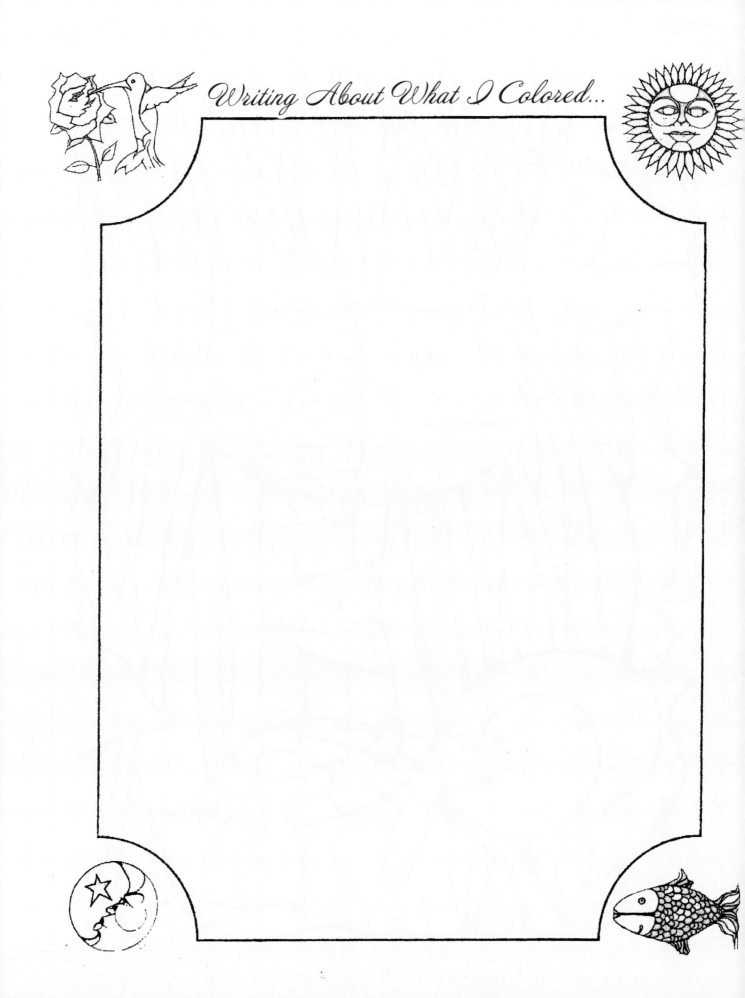

Writing About What I Colored...

Writing About What I Colored...

Writing About What I Colored...

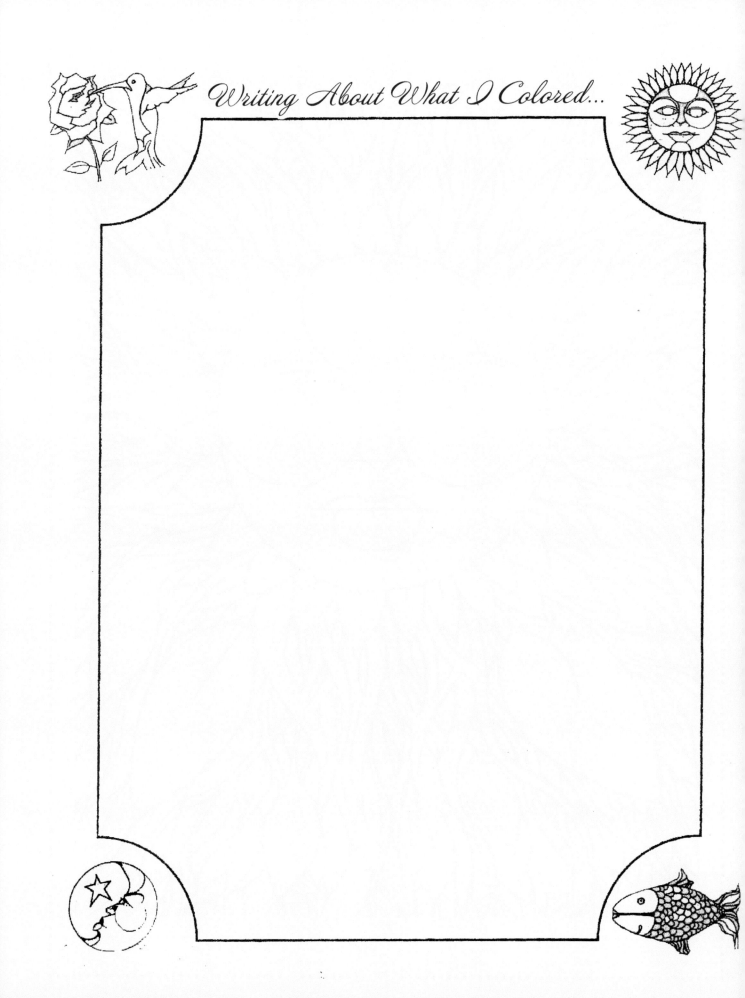

Writing About What I Colored...

Printed in the United States
By Bookmasters